WONDER WOMEN

HEROINES OF HISTORY

SACAGAWEA

NICOLE K. ORR

PURPLE TOAD PUBLISHING

Copyright © 2019 by Purple Toad Publishing, Inc. All rights reserved. No part of this book may be reproduced without written permission from the publisher. Printed and bound in the United States of America.

Printing   1   2   3   4   5   6   7   8   9

PUBLISHER'S NOTE
This series, Wonder Women: Heroines of History, covers racism and misogyny in United States history. Some of the events told in this series may be disturbing to young readers. The first-person narrative in chapter one of this book is a work of fiction based on the author's research.

Ida B. Wells
Nellie Bly
Sacagawea
Stagecoach Mary
Sybil Ludington

Library of Congress Cataloging-in-Publication Data
Orr, Nicole, K.
  Wonder Women: Sacagawea / Written by Nicole K. Orr.
    p. cm.
Includes bibliographic references, glossary and index.
ISBN 9781624694479
1. Sacagawea — Biography — Juvenile Literature. 2. — Lewis and Clark Expedition — Juvenile Literature. 3. Native Americans — Females — Juvenile Literature. I. Series: Wonder Women: Sacagawea
[B]
 TL797 .B55 A45 2019
 629.44/2

eBook ISBN: 9781624694462

Library of Congress Control Number 2018944211

ABOUT THE AUTHOR: Nicole K. Orr has been writing for as long as she's known how to hold a pen. She is the author of several other books by Purple Toad Publishing and has won National Novel Writing Month eleven times. Orr lives in Portland, Oregon, and camps under the stars whenever she can. When she isn't writing, she's flying to far-flung destinations around the world or taking road trips closer to home.

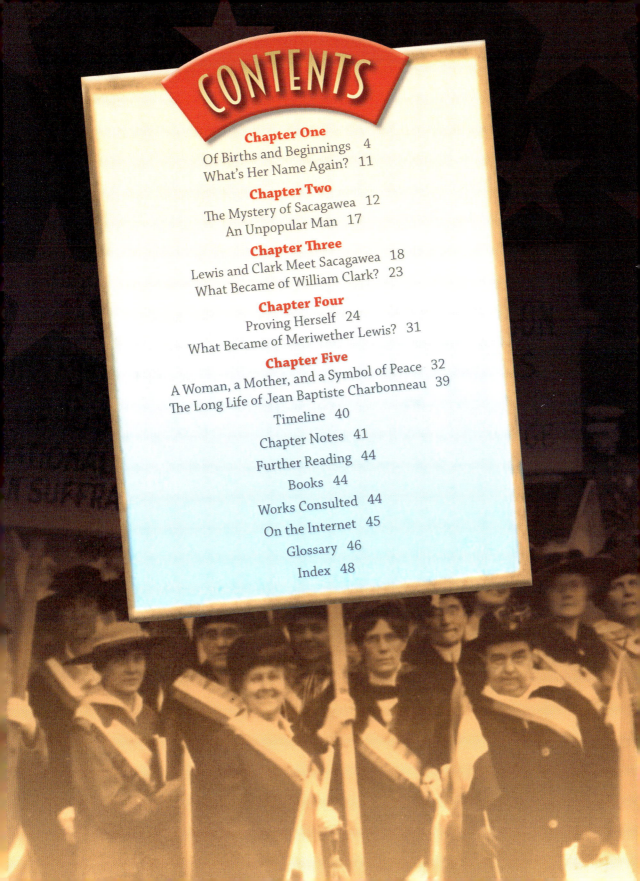

CONTENTS

Chapter One
Of Births and Beginnings 4
What's Her Name Again? 11

Chapter Two
The Mystery of Sacagawea 12
An Unpopular Man 17

Chapter Three
Lewis and Clark Meet Sacagawea 18
What Became of William Clark? 23

Chapter Four
Proving Herself 24
What Became of Meriwether Lewis? 31

Chapter Five
A Woman, a Mother, and a Symbol of Peace 32
The Long Life of Jean Baptiste Charbonneau 39

Timeline 40
Chapter Notes 41
Further Reading 44
Books 44
Works Consulted 44
On the Internet 45
Glossary 46
Index 48

OF BIRTHS AND BEGINNINGS

CHAPTER ONE

In my life, I have been taken captive by people in other Native American tribes. I was forced to marry a man I did not love. I was a guide and translator for a long expedition. I once dived into a river just to save important papers and journals. One of the most important things I've done in my life is give birth to my son. It was also one of the scariest.

When my son was ready to be born, we were at Fort Mandan in North Dakota, and it was not good timing. My husband, Toussaint Charbonneau, and I were going on an expedition in just two months. It was also winter and bitterly cold.

The labor was painful and lasted a very long time. I do not know what would have happened if I had been alone. It was lucky that Meriwether Lewis was there to help me. Later in the expedition, he would serve as a doctor for all of us, but he was a doctor first for me. He saw the terrible pain I was in and

While there are many statues of this incredible woman, the first one is located in Portland, Oregon, as part of the Lewis and Clark Exhibition. The statue was unveiled in 1905. The funds for it came from the National American Women's Suffrage Association.

CHAPTER ONE

Before Meriwether Lewis became a great explorer, he was President Jefferson's private secretary.

gave me something to help. He crushed the tails of rattlesnakes into a powder and then put the powder in water. He told me if I drank it, it would help the baby come.[1]

Not long after he gave me the rattlesnake water, my son came into the world. It was February 11, 1805, and we named him Jean Baptiste Charbonneau. While Lewis helped deliver my son, William Clark became like a father to him. He gave Jean Baptiste the nickname "Pomp," which means "firstborn" in the language of my people.

Other Shoshone mothers might have taken time to raise their new child at home, teach him the ways of the Shoshone, but I could not. Lewis and Clark were embarking on a journey, and they'd already waited long enough. We were in the Corps of Discovery, and we had to begin.

On April 7, two months after I had my son, we left Fort Mandan and began our journey. In order to bring Jean Baptiste along with me, I used a cradleboard. I wrapped him in a blanket and placed him on

OF BIRTHS AND BEGINNINGS

the board, then tied the leather straps to secure him. I could carry the cradleboard on my back, set it on the ground like a chair, or strap it to the side of a sled. It would keep him warm and keep him close, two very important things while we were traveling.[2]

As young as he was, Jean Baptiste helped the expedition. He reminded the men of their families back home. When people from other tribes saw us, they were not afraid. After all, no war party would travel with a woman and a child. Jean Baptiste became like a son to William Clark, so much so, Clark named a mountain after him. My son taught me a lesson as well. From him, I learned that sometimes the scariest and most painful experiences can provide the greatest rewards.

A child on a cradleboard. Lewis recorded a lot of things in his journals, including many of Sacagawea's Native American traditions.

7

CHAPTER ONE

Thomas Jefferson

As soon as she had started on the journey of motherhood, Sacagawea started a journey of exploration with Meriwether Lewis and William Clark. Lewis and Clark first met in 1795 when they served in the military. Sharing the same sense of curiosity, the two men quickly became friends.

In 1803, the United States bought a large section of land from France called the Louisiana Territory. President Thomas Jefferson was eager to have

At first, the borders of the Louisiana Purchase were unclear. Finally, in 1818 Great Britain and the United States agreed that the 49th parallel would be the dividing line between them. Everything north of that line would be Canada, which belonged to Great Britain.

OF BIRTHS AND BEGINNINGS

William Clark trusted the abilities of his slave, York, and brought him along on the trip. When Native American tribes met York, it was the first time they had seen someone with dark skin. Toward the end of the trip, the Corps of Discovery had to decide where to camp. Clark allowed York to vote, which historians believe was the first time an African American man was allowed to do so.

this area explored. He was especially hoping to find a route to the Pacific Ocean. To command this expedition, Jefferson selected his private secretary, Meriwether Lewis. Lewis couldn't undertake such a huge journey alone, so he brought on his friend William Clark.

When he accepted the offer, Clark wrote, " . . . my friend, I do assure you that no man lives whith whome I would perfur to undertake Such a Trip &c. as yourself."[3]

9

CHAPTER ONE

The 1954 postage stamp showing Lewis, Clark, and Sacagawea was made in honor of the 150th anniversary of the expedition.

Lewis and Clark would need more people on their team. By the time they were finished recruiting, more than two dozen men were ready to begin the adventure. At that time in history, it was not appropriate to include women. Sacagawea would be their only female member, but she would not be invited until several months after the Corps of Discovery set out.

WHAT'S HER NAME AGAIN?

When it comes to how her name is spelled and pronounced, historians do not all agree. One of the mysteries is who named her in the first place. Though she was born into a Shoshone tribe, she was not with them for very long before she was taken captive by the Hidatsa. Depending on which group of Native Americans named her, it would be spelled and pronounced differently. If the Hidatsa chose it for her, it would be spelled Sakakawea and means "bird woman." If the Lemhi Shoshone named her, it would be spelled Sacajawea, meaning "boat launcher" in the tribe's language. The most common spelling, however, is the one used in the journals of Lewis and Clark. It was Clark's opinion that Native American names should be spelled the way they are pronounced. Because of this, when he wrote down Sacagawea's name, he kept the "g" in it (sah-KOG-ah-WEE-ah). Over time, people began pronouncing the *g* like a *j* (sah-KAH-juh-WEE-uh). But even Lewis wasn't consistent. In his and Clark's journals, there are seven different spellings of her name.[4]

Sacagawea

The Mystery of Sacagawea

Chapter Two

Much of the beginning and ending of Sacagawea's life are a mystery. How she got her name, the year she was born, where she grew up, and the names of her parents are unknown. Despite this lack of information, people still find her fascinating. In fact, many historians are even more driven to find answers merely because so few have been found.

Sacagawea was born around 1788. Although the exact location of her birth is not clear, historians believe it was somewhere near Tendoy, Idaho. There, the Lemhi River runs between the Kenney Creek and Agency Creek. It was along the banks of this river that Sacagawea began her story.

The moment she entered the world, life was already difficult for her. She was born into the Shoshone nation, and the Shoshone were known to treat their women harshly. The boys were never beaten or punished. It was different with girls. They

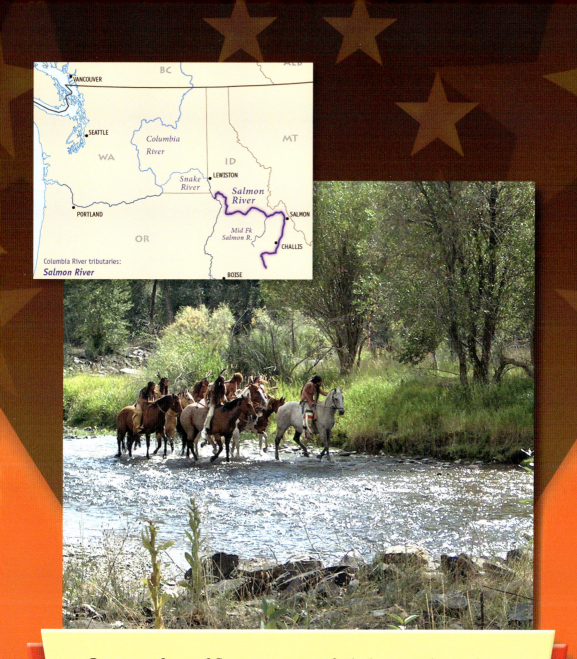

One way fans of Sacagawea can feel closer to her is by participating in a reenactment of the journey of the Corps of Discovery. The reenactment above is near the Lemhi River, which feeds the Salmon River, which feeds the Snake and Columbia Rivers.

CHAPTER TWO

A Lemhi chief and his wife from 1920. Today, there are fewer than 5300 Lemhi Shoshone.

were also given the worst jobs. Life became harder when the girls became women. The adult Shoshone males did the hunting and fighting. The adult Shoshone females handled everything else.

This lifestyle was normal for most Shoshone tribes, but Sacagawea's tribe, the Shoshone Lemhi, was different in some ways. They had been on the run for a long time. They were being chased through the wilderness by another tribe named the Hidatsa. Whenever the Hidatsa caught up with the Lemhi, they would steal their supplies and their food. The Lemhi were often starving and desperate. Members of the Lemhi often died because other members would not share food with them. There was very little loyalty among the Lemhi, and this made Sacagawea's childhood scary.

In the fall of 1800, when Sacagawea was about 12 years old, the Lemhi had run from Idaho and into Montana. Camped where several rivers came together with the Missouri River, the

Long Time Dog, a Hidatsa warrior

THE MYSTERY OF SACAGAWEA

Lemhi were attacked. The Hidatsa killed almost all of the Lemhi. Sacagawea and some other Shoshone women were taken captive. They were eventually sold to the Mandans, who kept Sacagawea and the other girls as slaves. In the 1800s, teenage girls could be forced to marry. In 1804, that's exactly what happened to 16-year-old Sacajawea.[1]

While some Native American tribes were enemies of others, many groups got along. They would trade with one another, which helped when winter came. They would also hold games and contests. Some of the contests were in hunting and dancing, for example. When games were hosted, there was very little to gamble with. Meat, clothing, and tools were three of the most popular goods added to

Native Americans and the shelters they used varied from tribe to tribe. This painting by George Catlin, titled *The Last Race, Mandan O-Kee-Pa Ceremony*, show the earth lodges in which the Mandan lived.

15

CHAPTER TWO

the wager. When men were out of these things, they would wager women or slaves.

French-Canadian trader Toussaint Charbonneau enjoyed these games. He often stayed with the Mandan while he traded animal furs. In 1804, he won Sacagawea in a game, and she became his property. He married her soon after, making her one of his wives.[2]

Toussaint Charbonneau was not a nice man. He was violent in how he spoke and moved. There was no one who knew this better than his wives. Sacagawea had gone from being hurt by the Lemhi to being kidnapped by the Hidatsa, and now she was married to a man who hurt her when he was angry. She did not know what it was like to be protected or treated with kindness.

She was about to find out. Lewis and Clark, two men who were very different from her husband, were in need of her and Charbonneau's talents.

Lewis and Clark did not have a quiet first meeting. In 1795, Lewis was a frontier army officer. He was court-martialed for challenging another man to a duel. The charges were dropped, but Lewis was still transferred to a different rifle company. There, he met his new superior, Commander William Clark.

AN UNPOPULAR MAN

History does not remember Toussaint Charbonneau well. Born around 1767, he was perhaps near 40 when he joined the Corps of Discovery. This made him the oldest member. He also lived longer than most of the men in the expedition. William Clark called Toussaint Charbonneau "a man of no particular merit," which meant that his bad qualities usually outweighed the good.[3] Lewis described him as "the most timid waterman in the world."[4] Historians have described him as big, arrogant, and mean. Movies and books call him a coward. During the expedition, he would hit Sacagawea if he became angry. Clark stepped in and stopped him at least once. It seems the only good thing Lewis and Clark's journals say of Charbonneau is that he was a great cook.

Charbonneau spent most of his life among Native Americans. He worked for fur trading companies, traveled between tribes, and was hired by the American government with Clark's help. By the time he died around 1843, Charbonneau had married at least five different Native American women; the youngest was 14 when he wed her. While he led a long life, Toussaint Charbonneau did not lead a popular one.[1]

Being a French-Canadian trader was dangerous work.

Lewis and Clark Meet Sacagawea

Chapter Three

All in all, the Lewis and Clark Expedition took three years and covered 8,000 miles. The trip went down the Ohio River, up the Missouri River, across the Continental Divide, and finally to the Pacific Ocean. The return trip followed a more southern route, using the Columbia River. The Corps of Discovery traveled by foot, boat, and horse. While Lewis and Clark had Sacagawea to thank for a lot of things, horses were one of the most important.

Even before the expedition began, Lewis and Clark knew they were going to need horses. President Jefferson couldn't provide them because the first part of the journey would be over water. The horses would be needed for the Bitterroot Mountains. The Shoshone who lived in that area were the only ones with horses.

Luckily enough for the expedition, the Corps already had a system to communicate with the Shoshone. First, Sacagawea would talk to the Native

Sacagawea leads Lewis and Clark through Three Forks, Montana, (above). The town was so honored to have played a role in the Corps of Discovery, they built the Sacagawea Hotel there in 1910.

CHAPTER THREE

Americans. Then she would translate what they said into the language of the Hidatsa. Third, her husband would take the Hidatsa words and switch them to French. Finally, since most members of the expedition spoke only English, François Labiche would translate the French message into English for Lewis and Clark.

On May 21, 1804, Lewis, Clark, and the other explorers left St. Louis, Missouri. They spent the first few months gathering supplies. In mid-August, the expedition met up with one of their first groups of Shoshone. Sacagawea met them and explained that they needed horses. She was delighted to see that the chief was, in fact, her brother Cameahwait. The meeting between siblings was short but joyous, and it was successful. The group now had horses.

A statue along the Missouri River commemorates where Lewis and Clark made one of their camps on their journey.

LEWIS AND CLARK MEET SACAGAWEA

Lewis and Clark approach a Mandan village. They logged discoveries like these in their journals.

It wasn't until November 2 that the expedition arrived in an area controlled by the Hidatsa. There, the expedition set up a temporary headquarters for the winter. They called it Fort Mandan.

At Fort Mandan, Lewis and Clark realized what they'd forgotten to bring. They had 200 pounds of gunpowder, 12 pounds of soap, and 193 pounds of portable soup. They did not, however, have a translator.[1]

On November 4, 1804, Toussaint Charbonneau and his pregnant wife, Sacagawea, arrived at Fort Mandan. They offered four buffalo robes to the men of the expedition. Charbonneau and Sacagawea knew several Native American languages, as well as French. Lewis and Clark asked the husband and wife to join them. They knew Charbonneau and Sacagawea would be a great help when the expedition met people from other tribes.

21

CHAPTER THREE

On February 11, 1805, Jean Baptiste Charbonneau was born. About two or three months later, the Corps of Discovery set out once more. There were two commanders, a full crew of men to assist them, three translators, and one baby.

Now, the real journey could begin.

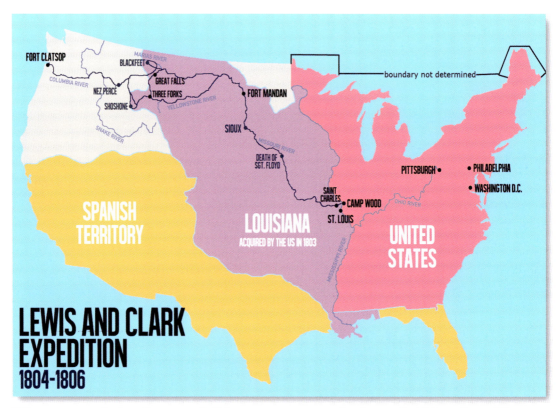

The route of the Corps of Discovery covered about 8,000 miles. The journals Lewis and Clark maintained during their journey detailed their expedition. Without those journals, it would be difficult to know exactly where the group camped, met with Native Americans, or how they survived disaster.

WHAT BECAME OF WILLIAM CLARK?

William Clark married twice and had more than seven children. He named his first child Meriwether Lewis Clark. In 1813, he was made governor of the Missouri Territory. In this role, Clark grew closer to Native American peoples and made friends with them. When they were forced to move from the Missouri Territory, Clark did his best to make it happen peacefully.

This friendship of Clark's began with Sacagawea and her son, whom he had nicknamed Pomp. During the expedition, Clark named a stone pillar Pompey's Tower. The rock, he reported, was "200 feet high 400 paces in [circumference] and only accessible on one side."[2] After the expedition, Pomp moved in with Clark and was treated like one of Clark's sons. A few years later, Sacagawea's other child, Lisette, joined Clark's household as well. At the end of his life, Clark moved in with his first son, Meriwether Lewis. He died there on September 1, 1838.

Meriwether Lewis Clark

PROVING HERSELF

CHAPTER FOUR

Lewis and Clark's journals, which they maintained throughout their journey, were important in many ways. They recorded every event, including illnesses, damage to boats, how much food they ate, and which tribes of Native Americans they met and how they were treated. The moment that Sacagawea earned respect from the men is also well documented in these journals.

The expedition used several different kinds of boats throughout the trip. When they left Fort Mandan with Sacagawea, they were using pirogues. To make them, cottonwood trees were cut down and the insides removed. These boats were very heavy. When the water dropped too low or even vanished altogether, the men would carry the boats. When the water was high enough again, they'd put the boats back in the river and continue on. This was a good routine and worked well when the weather was calm.

The pirogues that were used during the Corps of Discovery were heavy and sometimes difficult to carry over land. However, they could carry a lot of equipment.

CHAPTER FOUR

On May 16, 1805, a windstorm flipped one of the boats. Charbonneau and Sacagawea had been riding inside it, along with important documents, medicine, tools, and journals. Charbonneau could not swim, but his wife could. With her son strapped to her back, Sacagawea saved as many items as she could. This gained her the respect of the trip's two captains. In fact, they temporarily named a branch of the Missouri River after her.[1]

Soon, Sacagawea gained the respect of the rest of the men too. Since winter made hunting difficult, the Shoshone woman would gather berries and plants the men could eat instead. When the expedition came across new villages, even if

Sometimes the berries Sacagawea picked would be boiled down into a thick syrup. This would then be used to treat coughs and throats made sore by tuberculosis.

PROVING HERSELF

In this painting, *Lewis and Clark on the Lower Columbia*, by Charles M. Russell, Lewis and Clark reach the Columbia River on their way to the Pacific Ocean. They come upon a group of Native Americans whom Sacagawea greets with a show of peace.

Sacagawea did not know who lived in them, she'd walk out ahead of the men. With her son on her back, she would let the strangers see her and her child to show them that they were not a war party.

By the time they reached the Pacific Ocean on November 24, 1805, the members of the expedition had grown close. When the decision needed to be made where to spend the winter at the coast, Sacagawea and even Clark's slave York were allowed to vote. Fort Clatsop was created at what would later be called Astoria, Oregon. Fort Clatsop

27

CHAPTER FOUR

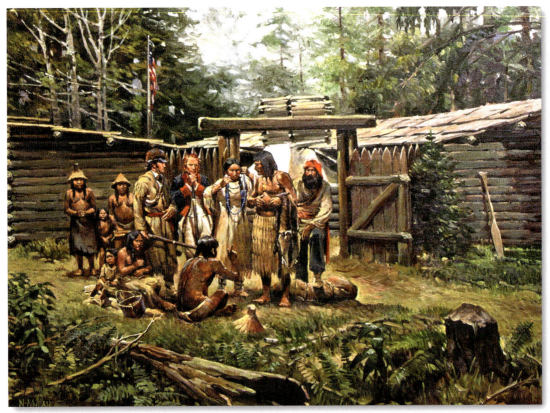

Fort Clatsop was a simple setup, but it was still a good place to rest and wait out the winter. The structure was just 50 feet wide, yet it provided shelter for the entire Corps of Discovery.

was intended to be used only until Lewis and Clark could find the right boats to take them back home. Unfortunately, they weren't able to find anything that could make the trip. Knowing they'd have to go back the way they came, they stole a canoe from a nearby Clatsop tribe and, on March 23, 1806, began retracing their steps.

The trip back was as complicated as the journey to the Pacific Ocean had been. First, the expedition had to get horses again. Second, they split into two groups. Clark took the route suggested by Sacagawea, which was a much safer choice. Lewis and his men followed another route, where Blackfeet attacked them. Everybody survived . . . at least on Meriwether Lewis' side. During the violence, two Blackfeet men were killed. This was the first time blood was shed from the western Native Americans by United States representatives. From this point on, there were never good relations between the Blackfeet and Americans. Later, Lewis and his men rode on to rejoin Clark.

When reconstruction began on Fort Mandan, the people involved wanted it to be as close to the original as possible. To that end, they used the blueprint that Clark had drawn on the cover of one of his journals.

CHAPTER FOUR

Only one man died on the entire expedition. Charles Floyd did not die of starvation or accident. His appendix ruptured. Even though they tried, there was nothing Lewis and Clark could have done for him.[2]

On August 14, Sacagawea and Charbonneau said their goodbyes at the place they'd joined the party: Fort Mandan. By September 3, 1806, the Corps of Discovery was back in St. Louis. The Lewis and Clark Expedition was officially over.

The Blackfeet were actually made up of four different tribes. These were the Southern Piegan, the Northern Piegan, the Kainai, and the Siksika.

WHAT BECAME OF MERIWETHER LEWIS?

After Lewis and Clark returned to St. Louis, Missouri, they were given money and land. When they traveled, everyone they met knew who they were. Meriwether Lewis was made governor of the Louisiana Territory. This did not work out well for him. It wasn't long before he was overwhelmed by the demands of the job. He was also trying to get his and Clark's journals published, but this was proving difficult too.

Even before the expedition, Lewis had had trouble with depression and drinking. When his journey was over, these became problems once again. On October 12, 1809, he died as a result of two gunshot wounds. He was 35 years old. At the time, the world considered it a suicide. In the years following, however, people have wondered if it was murder instead.[3]

Meriwether Lewis National Monument

31

A Woman, a Mother and a Symbol of Peace

Chapter Five

While the two years Sacagawea spent traveling with Lewis and Clark are well documented in the journals, the same does not apply to the years following the expedition. It is known that she and her husband returned to Fort Mandan on August 14, 1806. For the next three years, they lived among the Hidatsa, while Charbonneau sold furs.

When the expedition ended, Charbonneau was paid $500.33 and given 320 acres of land for his services. Sacagawea received no reward or payment at all. Sometime between 1810 and 1811, the couple moved to St. Louis to farm the land Charbonneau had been given. This did not last long. Charbonneau sold the land to Clark, who lived nearby, for $100. According to some reports, Charbonneau then worked for the Missouri Fur Company. He and Sacagawea went to live at Fort Manuel Lisa in South Dakota. There, Sacagawea gave birth to a daughter,

After the expedition, Charboneau and Sacagawea lived among the Hidatsa.

CHAPTER FIVE

Life in places like Fort Manuel Lisa might sound primitive to people now, but to people then, it meant a bed, a roof, and sometimes even a hot meal.

sometime in August 1812. By the age of two, Lisette had gone to live with Jean Baptiste and William Clark in St. Louis. Most historians believe that Lisette died before she was five years old.[1]

The date of Sacagawea's death is also uncertain. There are two theories. Sometime in December of 1812, one of Charbonneau's wives got sick and died. A man named John C. Luttig wrote in his journal, "This Evening the Wife of Charbonneau, a Snake Squaw, died of a putrid fever she was a good and the best Woman in the fort, aged abt. 25 years she left a fine infant girl."[2] This was considered proof that Sacagawea had died. More proof came when, on August 13, 1813, William Clark legally adopted both of Sacagawea's children. A long time after the Corps of Discovery finished their expedition, Clark wrote a list of the expedition's members. Next to Sacagawea's name, Clark wrote, "Dead."

The other theory claims Sacagawea died in 1875. Apparently, a Shoshone woman named Povio lived in Wyoming. Her sons were Baptiste and Bazil. She claimed she had gone along on Lewis and Clark's Expedition. These sons spoke both English and French. Her husband died first, and Povio died on April 9, 1884. This information did not come from Povio herself or from journals. It came from Dr.

A WOMAN, A MOTHER, AND A SYMBOL OF PEACE

Charles Eastman. In 1924, Eastman tried to solve the mystery of Sacagawea's death by interviewing Native Americans from many tribes. Everything known about Povio, including the possibility that she was Sacagawea, comes from Dr. Eastman's investigations.[3]

Charles Eastman was a prolific author and speaker on Sioux history and Native American history in general.

Regardless of when she died, most of the world agrees that Sacagawea was vital to the expedition's success. To honor her, there are lakes, mountains, rivers, schools, parks, and even a constellation named for her. In 2000, the U.S. Mint put her and her son on the gold dollar coin. There are countless books and movies about her. There is even a U.S. Navy ship with her name. There are more than 22 statues of Sacagawea in the world—more than of any other American woman. Many of these stand along the trail of the Corps of Discovery.

One statue, *Coming Home*, stands in Sacajawea Park in Three Forks, Montana. It is near where the young girl was taken captive by the Hidatsa. The plaque on the statue reads, "An Indian woman whose heroic courage, steadfast devotion and splendid loyalty in acting as Guide across the Rocky Mountains made it possible for the Lewis and

CHAPTER FIVE

Lewis and Clark memorial statue in Fort Benton, Montana

Clark Expedition to occupy so important a place in the history of this Republic."[4]

Because of the uncertainty about Sacagawea's death, there are two gravesites for her. The Wind River Indian Reservation in Wyoming marks where Povio died. Her marker, however, bears the name Sacagawea. In Mobridge, South Dakota, another marker bears her name. It is just 30 miles from Fort Manuel Lisa, where Sacagawea was last recorded to be.[5]

While Sacagawea was many things during the expedition, she later became a symbol of activism. She is seen as the face of female strength and courage. Many of the statues of Sacagawea were funded by women's rights groups.

As inspirational as her story is, much of what we know did not come from Sacagawea herself. As of 1902, Lewis and Clark were far better known than their translator. It was the book by Eva Emory Dye titled *The Conquest: The True Story of Lewis and Clark* that made

A WOMAN, A MOTHER, AND A SYMBOL OF PEACE

Sacagawea a true legend. Dye changed her story to make it more dramatic. Where Sacagawea's role had been as translator and peace symbol, Dye made her a guide. As fascination about Sacagawea grew, more pieces of the puzzle were put together, but there is still much more that people want to know.

Sacagawea led an eventful life. She was kidnapped from her tribe and forced to marry Toussaint Charbonneau. She joined an expedition of white men who were strangers. She raised her son while she traveled, protecting him from diseases, extreme weather, and starvation.

Although there are no known images of Sacagawea made during her lifetime, the statues and memorials she inspired will continue to remind us of her journey for generations to come.

CHAPTER FIVE

Even now, more than 200 years after the Corps of Discovery finished their epic trip, Sacagawea is still playing a role in the world. When people visit one of her statues, they will most likely think of her the way that she may have viewed herself: a mother, a woman, and a symbol of peace.

Sculptor Julia Davis created this statue of Sacagawea and Jean Baptiste. It stands in front of the Idaho Historical Museum in Boise, Idaho.

THE LONG LIFE OF JEAN BAPTISTE CHARBONNEAU

For the first six years or so of Jean Baptiste Charboneau's life, he went everywhere his mother did. After he was separated from Sacagawea sometime around 1810, he continued to travel, but did it alone. First, he moved in with William Clark and enrolled in the St. Louis Academy. There, the boy learned how to read and write, as well as how to speak English, French, and several Native American languages. In 1821, Jean Baptiste got his first job with the Missouri Fur Company. Two years later, he moved to Europe and learned to speak German and Spanish. Back in America, from 1829 to 1846, he worked for several different fur companies.

During the Mexican-American War (1846–1848), Jean Baptiste was made temporary mayor of Mission San Luis Rey de Francia. He left the position in 1848. By then, the Gold Rush was on. He spent the next decade looking for gold in what would later be Auburn, California.

He took a break from mining to become a manager at the Orleans Hotel, but in 1866 he returned to the gold hunt and set off for Montana. He did not make it. At age 61, he got sick and died. Jean Baptiste had gone from seeing the world from his mother's back to seeing the world himself. Most likely, his mother would have been proud.[6]

Jean Baptiste Charbonneau

TIMELINE

1767 Toussaint Charbonneau is born.

1788 Sacagawea is born somewhere in Idaho.

1795 Meriwether Lewis and William Clark meet for the first time.

1804 Charbonneau wins Sacagawea in a game. The Corps of Discovery officially sets out from St. Louis, Missouri.

1805 In February, Sacagawea gives birth to Jean Baptiste Charbonneau. The Corps of Discovery leaves Fort Mandan in April. On November 24, the Corps of Discovery arrives at the Pacific Ocean.

1806 Back at Fort Mandan, on August 14, Sacagawea and Charbonneau leave the expedition. Lewis and Clark return to St. Louis on September 23, finishing their journey..

1809 Meriwether Lewis dies on October 12 in Tennessee.

1812 Sacagawea gives birth to a daughter, Lisette.

1813 According to one theory, Sacagawea dies at Fort Mandan.

1838 William Clark dies.

1843? Toussaint Charbonneau dies.

1866 Jean Baptiste Charbonneau dies.

1869 The Transcontinental Railroad is completed.

1884 According to Dr. Charles Eastman's theory, Sacagawea dies in Wyoming.

CHAPTER NOTES

Chapter One

1. *This Day in History, 1805:* "Sacagawea Gives Birth to Pompey." History.com. http://www.history.com/this-day-in-history/sacagawea-gives-birth-to-pompey

2. Native Languages: "Native American Cradleboards." http://www.native-languages.org/cradleboard.htm

Sacagawea coin

41

CHAPTER NOTES

3. PBS. *Lewis & Clark: The Journey of the Corps of Discovery*. "Captain Meriwether Lewis." http://www.pbs.org/lewisandclark/inside/mlewi.html

4. History.com: "Lewis and Clark." http://www.history.com/topics/lewis-and-clark

Chapter Two

1. Sacajawea's Home: "Her Childhood." http://sacajaweahome.com/the-legend-of-her-name/her-childwood/

2. Ibid.

3. Discovering Lewis and Clark: "Toussaint Charbonneau." http://www.lewis-clark.org/article/2664

4. Ibid.

Chapter Three

1. PBS. *Lewis & Clark: The Journey of the Corps of Discovery*. "To Equip an Expedition." http://www.pbs.org/lewisandclark/inside/idx_equ.html

2. *Lewis & Clark Expedition*. "Pompey's Pillar." National Park Service. Unknown date. https://www.nps.gov/nr/travel/lewisandclark/pom.htm

Chapter Four

1. Sacagawea Historical Society: "Sacagawea's Role and Significance in the Lewis and Clark Expedition." http://www.sacagawea-biography.org/significance-role-lewis-clark-expedition/

CHAPTER NOTES

2. PBS. *Lewis & Clark: The Journey of the Corps of Discovery.* "Sergeant Charles Floyd." http://www.pbs.org/lewisandclark/inside/cfloy.html
3. *This Day in History, 1809*: "Meriwether Lewis Dies Along the Natchez Trace, Tennessee." History.com. http://www.history.com/this-day-in-history/meriwether-lewis-dies-along-the-natchez-trace-tennessee

Chapter Five

1. *Native Americans: The True Story of Sacagawea and Her People.* "What Happened After the Expedition Returned?" http://bonniebutterfield.com/sacagawea-death.html
2. Ibid.
3. Sacagawea Historical Society: "Controversy of Sacagawea's Death." http://www.sacagawea-biography.org/controversy-of-death/
4. *Sacagawea: Master Explorer*: "The Landmarks." 2017. https://commons.marymount.edu/jowetttopic/the-landmark/
5. Ibid.
6. Sacagawea Historical Society: "Jean Baptiste Charbonneau, 'Pomp.'" http://www.sacagawea-biography.org/jean-baptiste-charbonneau-pomp/

FURTHER READING

Books

Frazier, Neta Lohnes. *Path to the Pacific: The Story of Sacagawea.* London: Young Voyageur, 2016.

Jazynka, Kitson. *National Geographic Readers: Sacagawea.* Washington, DC: National Geographic Children's Books, 2015.

Krull, Kathleen. *Women Who Broke the Rules: Sacajawea.* New York: Bloomsbury USA Children's, 2015.

Maguire, Amy Jane. *The Indian Girl Who Led Them, Sacajawea.* London: Forgotten Books, 2015.

Mead, Maggie. *Exploring the West: Tales of Courage on the Lewis and Clark Expedition.* South Egremont, MA: Red Chair Press, 2015.

Works Consulted

Andrews, Evan. "10 Little-Known Facts About the Lewis and Clark Expedition." History.com. November, 2015. http://www.history.com/news/history-lists/10-little-known-facts-about-the-lewis-and-clark-expedition

Harvey, Ian. "Interesting Facts You Didn't Know About the Lewis and Clark Expedition." *The Vintage News.* July, 2016. https://www.thevintagenews.com/2016/07/27/unknown-facts-lewis-clarks-expedition/

History.com: "Sacagawea" http://www.history.com/topics/native-american-history/Sacagawea

FURTHER READING

Lewis and Clark's Historic Trail
   https://lewisclark.net/
Lewisclark.net.
   https://lewisclark.net/
Monticello
   http://www.monticello.org
PBS. *Lewis & Clark: The Journey of the Corps of Discovery*.
   http://www.pbs.org/lewisandclark/
Sacagawea Historical Society
   http://www.sacagawea-biography.org
Sacagawea: Master Explorer
   https://commons.marymount.edu/jowetttopic/

On the Internet
Ducksters: Sacagawea
   http://www.ducksters.com/biography/explorers/sacagawea.php
History.com: Sacagawea
   http://www.history.com/topics/native-american-history/sacagawea
National Geographic: Lewis and Clark
   https://www.nationalgeographic.com/lewisandclark/

GLOSSARY

activism (AK-teh-VIZ-em)—Working for social or political change.

arrogance (AH-roh-gans)—An elevated sense of one's own importance or abilities.

constellation (CON-stuh-LAY-shun)—A group of stars that form a clear pattern.

expedition (ex-puh-DIH-shun)—A journey undertaken by a group of people with a specific goal.

gamble (GAM-bul)—To bet items or money against a certain outcome in a game.

infant (IN-fint)—A baby.

labor (LAY-bohr)—The process of childbirth.

mining (MY-ning)—To dig for coal or other minerals.

recruiting (ree-KROOT-ing)—To bring new people into a group or cause.

reenactment (re-en-AKT-mint)—To act out a past event.

rupture (RUP-shur)—To burst.

squaw (SKAHW)—A Native American woman or wife.

timid (TIH-mid)—A lack of courage or confidence.

GLOSSARY

Jean Baptiste Charboneau historical marker

translator (TRANZ-lay-tur)—A person who takes words in one language and makes them another.

tuberculosis (to-bur-kyoo-LOH-sus)—A disease of the lungs.

value (VAL-yoo)—The worth of something, usually based on money.

PHOTO CREDITS: Cover, pp. 6, 8, 9, 10, 14, 15, 17, 18, 26, 27, 30, 32, 33, 34, 39—Public Domain; p. 1—Jason Turgeon; p. 4—Julie; p. 7—Vanessa Roanhorse; p. 11—Leonard Crunelle; p. 13—PFly, BLMidaho; p. 16—Bill McChesney; p. 20—Patrick Emerson; p. 21—US Capitol; p. 22—Carte; p. 23—Thomas M. Easterly; p. 25—Basile Morin; p. 28—Don Graham; p. 29—Chris Light; p. 30—Skye Marthaler; p. 35—Jerrye and Roy Klotz MD; p. 37—Nathan Borror; p. 38—cifraserl; p. 41—Matthias; p. 47—Jeffery G. Backes. Every measure has been taken to find all copyright holders of material used in this book. In the event any mistakes or omissions have happened within, attempts to correct them will be made in future editions of the book.

INDEX

Bazil 34

Blackfeet 28–29, 30

Cameahwait 20

Charbonneau, Jean Baptiste (Pomp) 4, 6, 7, 22, 23, 27, 34, 35, 38, 39, 47

Charboneau, Lisette 34

Charbonneau, Toussaint 4, 16, 17, 21, 26, 29, 32, 34, 38

Clark, William 6, 7, 8, 9, 10, 11, 16, 17, 18, 19, 20, 21, 23, 24, 27, 28, 29, 31, 32, 34, 37, 39,

Conquest: The True Story of Lewis and Clark, The 37

Dye, Eva Emory 37

Eastman, Charles 35

Floyd, Charles 29

Fort Clatsop 27, 28

Fort Mandan 4, 6, 21, 24, 29, 32

Fort Manuel Lisa 34, 36

Hidatsa 11, 14, 15, 16, 20, 21, 32, 33, 35

horses 18, 20, 28

Jefferson, Thomas 8, 9, 18

Labiche, Francois 20, 22

Lewis, Meriwether 4, 6, 7, 8, 9, 10, 11, 16, 17, 18, 19, 20, 21, 23, 24, 27, 28, 29, 31, 37

Luttig, John C. 34

Pompey's Tower 23

Povio 34, 35, 36

Sacagawea
   as guide 4
   birth 12
   children 4, 6, 7, 22, 23, 27, 34, 35, 38, 39
   coin 35
   death 34, 35, 36
   in captivity 4
   marriages 4
   names 11, 12
   stamp 10
   statues 5, 11, 20, 35-36, 37, 38

Sacagawea Hotel 19

Three Forks, Montana 19, 35

York 9, 27